Fangs
DEATH ADDERS

Super Deadly!

by Nancy White

Consultant: Raoul Bain, Biodiversity Specialist, Herpetology
Center for Biodiversity and Conservation
American Museum of Natural History
New York, New York

BEARPORT
PUBLISHING

New York, New York

Credits

Cover and Title Page, © Barry Hatton; TOC, © Ken Griffiths/NHPA/Photoshot; 4, © Bill Bachman/Alamy; 5, © Pavel German; 7, © Steven David Miller/Animals Animals Enterprises; 8L, © Mark O'Shea/NHPA/Photoshot; 8M, © Ralph & Daphne Keller/NHPA/Photoshot; 8R, © Greg Harold/Auscape; 9, © Ted Mead/ANTphoto; 10, © Ken Griffiths/NHPA/Photoshot; 11, © Michael & Patricia Fogden/Corbis; 12, © Ken Griffiths/NHPA/Photoshot; 13, © NHPA/Photoshot; 14, © Adam Elliott/OzImages International; 15, © Ken Griffiths/ANTphoto; 16, © Jason Edwards/National Geographic/Getty Images; 17, © Photography ebiz; 18, © Adam Elliott/OzImages International; 19, © John Carnemolla/Auscape; 20, © Robert Valentic/Nature Picture Library; 21, © Rod Williams/gekkoimages; 22, © Ian Waldie/Getty Images; 23A, © Bill Bachman/Alamy; 23B, © IntraClique/Shutterstock; 23C, © Greg Harold/Auscape; 23D, © Photocyclops.com/SuperStock; 23E, © Snowleopard1/Shutterstock; 23F, © Maria Dryfhout/Shutterstock; 23G, © Snowleopard1/Shutterstock; 23H, © Susan Flashman/Shutterstock

Publisher: Kenn Goin
Senior Editor: Lisa Wiseman
Creative Director: Spencer Brinker
Photo Researcher: Q2A Media: Poulomi Basu
Cover Design: Dawn Beard Creative

Library of Congress Cataloging-in-Publication Data

White, Nancy, 1942-
  Death adders : super deadly! / by Nancy White.
    p. cm. — (Fangs)
  Includes bibliographical references and index.
  ISBN-13: 978-1-59716-764-2 (library binding)
  ISBN-10: 1-59716-764-9 (library binding)
  1. Acanthophis—Juvenile literature. I. Title.

  QL666.O64W448 2009
  597.96'4—dc22

                          2008037180

For more information, write to Bearport Publishing Company, Inc., 101 Fifth Avenue, Suite 6R, New York, New York 10003. Printed in the United States of America.

10 9 8 7 6 5 4 3 2 1

Contents

The Hidden Killer

On a hot afternoon in the Australian **bush**, nothing is moving. There's not a living creature in sight. Yet one of the world's deadliest snakes lies hidden among the leaves and rocks, waiting for its next meal.

Suddenly, some hikers come along, unaware of the hidden danger. One of them steps on the snake and it **strikes**, leaving two small holes on his ankle. The hiker realizes a death adder has bitten him. Soon his eyelids begin to droop, and he feels weak and dizzy. In a few hours, he won't be able to move, speak, or open his eyes. Luckily, a special medicine can save his life.

▲ Hikers in the Australian bush

death adder

Death adders grow to be about 19 to 35 inches (48 to 89 cm) long.

The Most Dangerous

Death adders are one of the most dangerous snakes in the world. They belong to a group of **venomous** snakes called elapids (EL-uh-pidz). King cobras, coral snakes, and black mambas are also part of this family.

Even though a death adder is an elapid, it looks different from the other members of its family. Its relatives have small, narrow heads, short **fangs**, and thin bodies covered with smooth **scales**. The death adder, however, has a large triangle-shaped head and long fangs. Its body is wide, and it has a thin, rat-like tail.

▲ Death adders are found only in Australia, Indonesia, and Papua New Guinea. They usually make their homes in places where people don't live.

triangle-shaped
head

wide body

rat-like tail

There are at least three different types of death adders. Their shape makes it easy to see where their bodies end and their tails begin.

An Invisible Cloak

Not all death adders are the same color. They can be red, brown, gray, green, or yellow. Their bellies are light-colored and sometimes have dark spots. These snakes can have yellow or white stripes around their bodies, too.

The death adder's body colors are very important. They help protect the snake from enemies. When it hides among leaves and rocks, its colors blend in so that its body can't be seen. This is called **camouflage**. It's as if the snake is wearing a cloak that makes it invisible.

Death adders come in many different colors.

8

A death adder
camouflaged by
grass and sand

The only part of the
death adder's body
that doesn't have camouflage
colors is its tail.

Mysterious Moves

Camouflage helps many animals hunt for **prey**. It allows them to move close to their **victims** without being seen.

A death adder, however, doesn't chase its prey. It hunts by hiding and waiting. When it's hungry, the snake finds a place to hide, usually among rocks or leaves. Its colors make it hard for other animals to spot it. Next, the death adder curls itself into a horseshoe shape with its head and tail facing each other. Then it raises just the tip of its tail and wiggles it. Why?

▲ A death adder curls its body into a horseshoe shape as it waits for prey.

Lying in wait for prey instead of going out to find a meal is called ambush hunting. The word *ambush* means a surprise attack from a hiding place.

A Tricky Tail

The snake's tail is a trap. While it can easily be seen by other animals, it doesn't look like a tail. It looks more like a worm or a caterpillar—just the kind of little creature a lizard, frog, mouse, or bird would eat.

When an animal sees the wiggling tail, it often comes closer, thinking it's going to get a tasty meal. Instead, it has a surprise coming. The animal is going to *be* the meal!

tail

The death adder will not strike until it knows its prey is close enough for it to bite on the first try. If it misses, the prey will have a chance to escape, and the snake might not be able to catch it. Death adders are tricky, but they're not very fast.

frog

The Jaws of Death

As the death adder's tail keeps wiggling, the victim moves closer and closer. Soon the animal is near enough to snap at the tail. Before it has a chance, however, the deadly killer lashes out, with open jaws and needle-sharp fangs.

The snake sinks its fangs into the victim's flesh, pumping deadly venom into the struggling animal. It holds on until the struggle stops and the victim goes limp. Then the death adder slowly swallows its meal whole.

fangs

The death adder has the quickest strike of any snake in the world. It can strike, bite, and curl up again in less than one tenth of one second. That's about as long as it takes to blink an eye!

Undercover

Death adders are clever killers. Yet even they can be killed! Foxes, wild cats, and some large birds kill and eat them. Another animal called the cane toad likes to eat death adder babies.

Luckily for the snake, camouflage helps protect it from enemies. When it's resting during the day, the death adder stays under leaves and rocks. It doesn't stick out its tail, as it does when it's lying in wait for prey. It keeps its whole body well hidden. The creature is almost impossible to see.

cane toad

Death adders stay hidden most of the day, resting or waiting for prey. After dark, when they can't be seen, they come out and move around. However, these snakes don't travel when the moon is full. Enemies would be able to see them in the bright moonlight.

death adder

Humans, Beware!

Death adders are so good at hiding that people hardly ever see them. Yet these snakes have a habit that's very dangerous to humans. Unlike most venomous snakes, they don't slither away if a person comes near. They stay put.

If a hiker walks up to one without seeing it, the snake won't budge. If the person accidentally steps on it or if the snake thinks the person's foot is prey, it will bite!

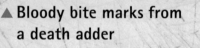

▲ Bloody bite marks from a death adder

Half the people bitten by death adders die within 48 hours, unless they get a shot of a special medicine called antivenin (*an*-tee-VEN-uhn). Amazingly, the medicine is made from the death adder's venom.

Venom is being taken from this death adder in order to make antivenin. This process is called milking.

Small but Deadly

Like most other snakes, death adder babies come out of eggs. However, the eggs don't leave the mother's body until the babies are ready to hatch. The shells are so thin that the babies can easily break through.

More than 20 baby death adders may be born at one time. Soon after birth, the young snakes start wiggling their tricky tails. When prey comes along, they'll strike with lightning speed and kill with their super-deadly venom—just like their parents.

▲ Death adder babies hatching

Death adder babies are only about six inches (15 cm) long. It takes two or three years for them to be fully grown. These snakes can live to be 30 years old.

Fang Facts

- Unlike most elapids, a death adder is able to move its fangs. The snake aims them forward as it strikes at its prey.

- A death adder's fangs can fall out. When this happens, new fangs grow in their place. The snake often swallows its old fangs.

fangs

▲ Death adder

- The strength of a snake's venom is often measured by how many mice the venom from one bite can kill. One bite from a death adder can kill more than 2,000 mice! This makes the death adder one of the ten most dangerous snakes in the world.

- People who are bitten by death adders may not feel anything at first, but soon they're in pain. Their eyelids begin to droop, and they feel weak and dizzy. After about six hours, they can't move, speak, or open their eyes. Their breathing becomes very slow. However, a shot of antivenin can help them survive. The shot should be given at the first sign of weakness, but it can help even if it's given later on.